A Day in the Life Of

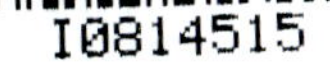

An Ant

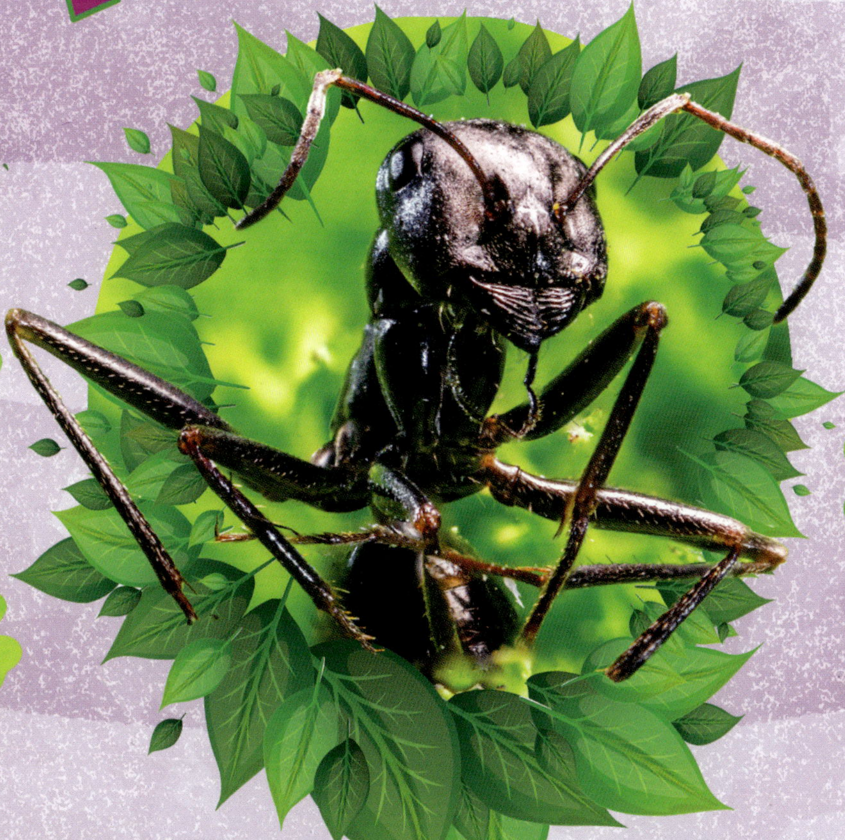

Ruby Tuesday Books

Ruth Owen

Published in 2025 by Ruby Tuesday Books Ltd.

Editor: Mark J. Sachner
Design: Tammy West
Production: John Lingham

Photo Credits:
Alamy: 11 (Biosphoto), 12 (Hakan Soderholm), 19 (Antje Schulte/Ant Life); iStock: 7 (Istvan Balogh), 8–9 (samuiboy), 13B (Lucia Ghetti); Nature Picture Library: 10 (Rod Williams), 15 (Stephen Dalton); Science Photo Library: 17 (Clouds Hill Imaging); Shutterstock: Cover (Dmitry Dolhikh), 4 (Rupendra Singh Rawat), 5 (Ksenia Lada), 6 (Yeti Studio & PaulrommerSL), 13T (Inga Nielsen), 16 (ABO Photography), 20 (Photo Fun), 21 (Maximillian cabinet), 22 (Dwi Yulianto, Anton Kozyrev, & Irina Kozorog), 23 (Catcher of Light Inc, irin-k, & Jirasak Kaewtongsorn), 24 (K.IvanS); Kamil Stajniak: 14; Superstock: 18 (Matt Cole).

Library of Congress Control Number: 2024941194

Print (Hardback) ISBN 978-1-78856-492-2
Print (Paperback) ISBN 978-1-78856-493-9
ePub ISBN 978-1-78856-494-6

Published in Minneapolis, MN
Printed in the United States

www.rubytuesdaybooks.com

CONTENTS

Meet a Busy Worker Ant

It's morning in a backyard.

A black garden ant and her family leave their underground nest.

She is a worker ant, and her job is to find food.

The ant uses her two **antennae** to smell for food.

The ant finds sugary candy that was dropped by a human.

She scurries back to the nest.

Her body makes a special smelly **trail**.

Other worker ants follow her trail to eat the candy.

The little worker ant finds a dead millipede.

This **HUGE** meal needs teamwork!

The ant makes a smelly trail back to the nest.

A team of ants comes to carry the millipede back to their home.

Thousands of ants live in the nest.

The worker ants must find lots of food for their family.

When they need a drink, the ants sip water from raindrops.

The ant makes a trail from something sweet on the backyard deck.

The ant has two **stomachs.** One is for the food she eats.

Her second stomach is for food she carries back to the nest.

Back at their underground nest, the ants spit up the food they collect.

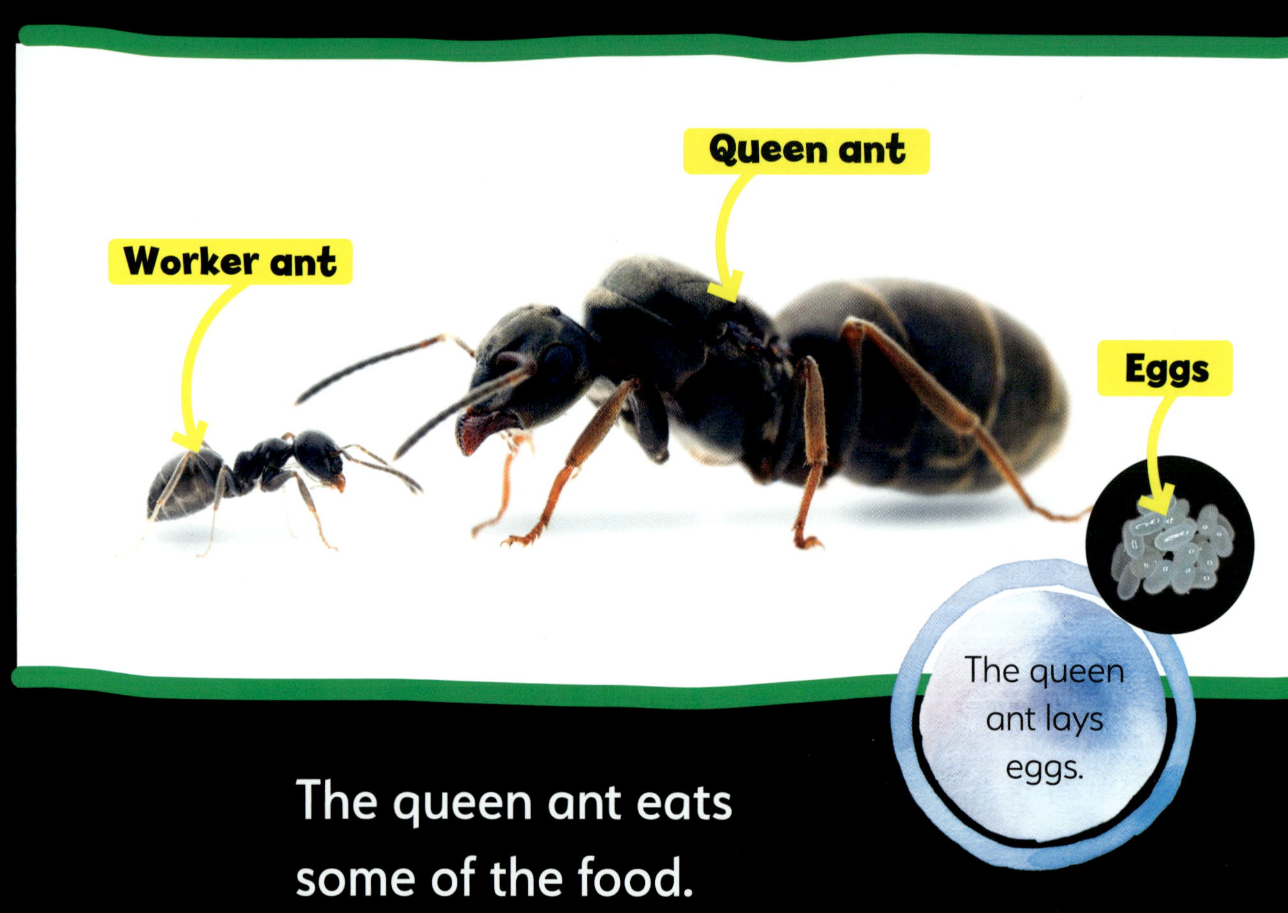

The queen ant lays eggs.

The queen ant eats some of the food.

She is the mother of all the ants.

Workers in the nest also feed the food to the baby ants.

A baby ant is called a **larva**.

The busy worker ant has another way to get food.

With the other workers, she takes care of little **insects** called aphids.

Aphids suck a sugary juice called sap from plants.

A close-up picture of an aphid

The worker ant tickles an aphid with her antennae.

This makes the aphid poop out sweet stuff called honeydew.

The worker ant gobbles up the honeydew.

Ladybugs and other insects eat aphids.

The worker ants protect their aphids from these **predators**.

The ants bite the hungry ladybug.

When evening comes, the little ant goes underground.

Tomorrow will be another busy day!

Glossary

antennae
Two long body parts on the head of an insect. Antennae may be used for touching, smelling, and tasting.

insect
A tiny animal with six legs. Ants, ladybugs, beetles, and bees are all insects.

larva
A young insect that hatches from an egg.

predator

An animal that hunts and eats other animals.

stomach

A bag-like body part where food goes after it's eaten by a person or animal.

trail

A pathway that can be followed. A trail might be marked with signs. Some animals use smell to mark a trail.

Index